MOUNTAIN MADNESS

Contents

Haydn Middleton

Story illustrated by Seb Burnett

Before Reading

In this story

 Schoolboy Mo who is also Mole Man

 The Big Slug, his arch enemy

 Captain Yak

Tricky words

- obstacle
- twitching
- special
- ordinary
- Himalayas
- Mount Everest
- roller-coaster
- avalanche

Introduce these tricky words and help the reader when they come across them later!

Story starter

Mo is no ordinary boy. He has a very special nose and when he smells trouble, something amazing happens – Mo turns into a super-hero called Mole Man! On Sports Day, Mo was getting ready for the obstacle race when he smelled bad trouble.

Mole Man
Up Mount Everest

It was Sports Day at Mo's school.

Everyone was getting ready.

"I will be in the obstacle race," said Mo.

"I'm good at going through tunnels."

Just then his nose started twitching.

Mo had a special nose. He could smell trouble anywhere in the world. And he smelled *bad* trouble now. "Please can I get some water?" asked Mo, and he ran off.

Mo rushed to his secret spot – and he burst out of his PE kit.

Mo was not an ordinary boy any more.

Mo was now ... **Mole Man**!

"Sniff, sniff," went Mole Man.

"Time to go digging."

So Mole Man set off underground
to find the trouble.

He dug faster than the speed of light!

Mole Man dug under land and sea.

"I bet the Big Slug is behind this trouble," he said. "But Mole Man can sort it out."

Soon his nose was twitching really fast.

"Sniff, sniff," went Mole Man.

"Time to tunnel *up*."

A moment later he burst up
through the ground. He was in
the Himalayas, next to Mount Everest.
A huge sheet of snow and ice
was hanging off Mount Everest.

"Mole Man!" cried Captain Yak. "You've come at just the right time! We're in terrible trouble. The Big Slug is making a theme park. He is turning Mount Everest into a roller-coaster ride and it's making an avalanche!"

"Sniff," went Mole Man.

"I thought I smelled the Big Slug and I saw the avalanche. Tell all your yaks to come here."

"*All* of them?" asked Captain Yak.

"All of them," said Mole Man.

"I'm going to tunnel up Mount Everest."

Up, up, up Mole Man dug – right to the top of Mount Everest.
There was the Big Slug with all his slug-helpers, making the roller-coaster.
Mole Man turned around and went back down his tunnel.

Why did the Big Slug choose Mount Everest for his roller-coaster?

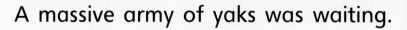

A massive army of yaks was waiting.

"Excellent!" said Mole Man.

"Now what can we all do?" asked Captain Yak.

"Tell all your yaks to dig their horns under the roller-coaster track and push it up!" said Mole Man.

It was amazing! The yaks pushed as hard as they could. They pushed and pushed and the track began to lift. Slowly it went up and up.

At the top of Mount Everest the Big Slug got on to the ride.
"My roller-coaster is going to be the fastest ride in the world," he said, as he zoomed down the track.

Then the Big Slug saw that the track was not going down any more.
It was going up!
"This must be the work of Mole Man," he cried. "I'm coming to get you!"
But the Big Slug couldn't stop!
"Enjoy your ride!" called Mole Man.

The yaks pushed away all the track and the avalanche was stopped.
"Thanks, Mole Man!" said Captain Yak.
"No problem!" said Mole Man.
Then he dug all the way back to school and changed into his PE kit.

Mo rushed back to the obstacle race.

"Just in time," said his teacher.

"Where on Earth have you been?"

"Just to Mount Everest," said Mo.

His teacher smiled.

"You and your little stories," he said.

Quiz

Text Detective

- How did Mole Man plan to stop the Big Slug?
- Why do you think Mo chose the obstacle race?

Word Detective

- Phonic Focus: Doubling consonants
  Page 3: What must be added to 'get' before adding 'ing'?
- Page 12: Find a word meaning the opposite of 'quickly'.
- Page 16: Which words does Mo say?

Super Speller

Read these words:

getting   soon   under

Now try to spell them!

HA! HA! HA!

Q What do you say when you meet a mountain?

A High!

17

Before Reading

Find out about

- People who climb up Mount Everest – to the top of the world!

Tricky words

- mountains
- Himalayas
- measured
- climbers
- oxygen
- breathe
- Sherpas

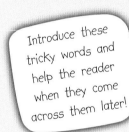

Introduce these tricky words and help the reader when they come across them later!

Text starter

Mount Everest in the Himalayas is the highest place on Earth. Many climbers have tried to reach the top of Everest. Local people called Sherpas help the climbers. Climbing Everest is very dangerous, and many people have died.

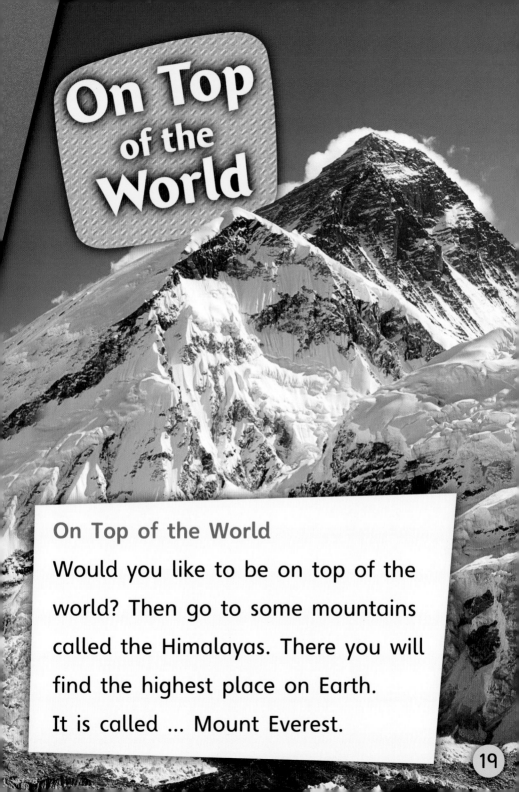

On Top of the World

On Top of the World

Would you like to be on top of the world? Then go to some mountains called the Himalayas. There you will find the highest place on Earth.
It is called ... Mount Everest.

How High is Mount Everest?

It is hard to say just how high Mount Everest is.

No one has measured Mount Everest with a tape measure!

But it is about 9,000 metres – or **5 miles** – high!

Many climbers have tried to climb
Everest. They dreamed of getting right
to the top.

They wanted to be on top of the world.

But Everest is covered in ice and snow
and many climbers have died there.

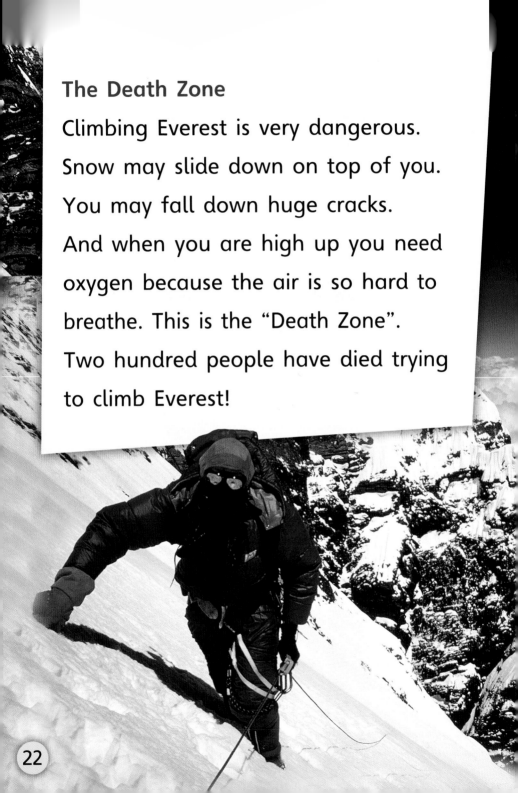

The Death Zone

Climbing Everest is very dangerous.
Snow may slide down on top of you.
You may fall down huge cracks.
And when you are high up you need
oxygen because the air is so hard to
breathe. This is the "Death Zone".
Two hundred people have died trying
to climb Everest!

Local people called Sherpas help climbers on Everest.

There are no roads to Everest so the Sherpas use yaks to bring the food, ropes and ladders to the mountain.

Then the Sherpas carry the food, ropes and ladders *up* Everest.

Did he get to the top?

The year was 1924.

No one had ever got all the way to the top of Everest. Then a British climber called George Mallory set off.

Someone below said he saw Mallory right at the top.

But Mallory never came back down.

Mallory's grandson climbed Everest in 1995.

In 1999, climbers found Mallory's body.
It was very near the top.
But when he died, was he climbing up or down?
Was he the first person to reach the top of Everest?

They did it!

The year was 1953.

Still no climber had reached the top
of Everest and come back down.

Then at last someone did.

And not just one climber did it,
but two! They were Edmund Hillary,
from New Zealand, and Tenzing Norgay,
a Sherpa.

But who was the **very** first climber
at the top of Everest?
Was it Hillary or Tenzing?
At first, they would not say.
Then at last Tenzing said it was Hillary!

More and more climbers

After that, more climbers got to the top.
More climbers died too.
Fifteen climbers died in just one year.
But some amazing climbers did go
all the way to the top.

In 1970, Yuichiro Miura of
Japan got to the top –
then he **skied** all the way down!

In 1996, Goran Kropp rode from Sweden to Everest on a bike.
Then he climbed to the top of Everest. And *then* he rode his bike all the way home again!

In 1998, Tom Whittaker climbed Everest, but he had only one real leg! He was the first disabled climber to reach the top.

In 2004, Sherpa Pemba Dorji reached the top in just 8 hours 10 minutes! He used ropes and ladders left by other climbers.
Back in 1953, Hillary and Tenzing had to take their own ropes and ladders. It took *them* 7 weeks!

Quiz

Text Detective

- What is the name of the highest mountain in the world?
- Would you like to climb Mount Everest?

Word Detective

- **Phonic Focus:** Doubling consonants
  Page 24: What must be added to 'set' before adding 'ing'?
- Page 19: How do you know which words are the title?
- Page 26: Why do Edmund Hillary and Tenzing Norgay have capital letters?

Super Speller

Read these words:

carry   near   setting

Now try to spell them!

HA! HA! HA!

Q Where do snowmen go to dance?

A The snowball.